STRUM & SING

CAMPFIRE FOLK SONGS

Cherry Lane Music Company
Director of Publications: Mark Phillips

ISBN 978-1-57560-717-7

Visit our website at www.cherrylane.com

CONTENTS

All My Trials

African-American Spiritual

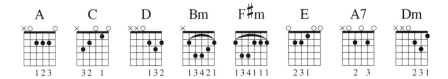

A   C   D   Bm   F♯m   E   A7   Dm

Verse 1

A | **|C** |
If religion was a thing that money could buy,

|A | **|D** **|Bm** ‖
The rich would live and the poor would die.

Chorus

A **|F♯m** **|Bm** | |
All   my trials, Lord,

E | **|A** | |
Soon   be over.

A | **|A7** **|Dm** | |
Too late, my brothers, too late, but never mind.

A **|F♯m** **|Bm** | |
All   my trials, Lord,

E | **|A** | ‖
Soon   be over.

Repeat Chorus

Verse 2

    A | |**C** |
    I had a little book, 'twas given to me,

    |**A** | |**D** |**Bm** ||
    And every page spelled "Victo - ry."

Repeat Chorus

Verse 3

    A | |**C** |
    Hush, little baby, don't you cry.

    |**A** | |**D** |**Bm** ||
    You know your momma was born to die.

Repeat Chorus

Blowin' in the Wind

Words and Music by Bob Dylan

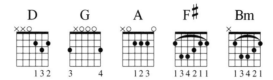

Verse 1

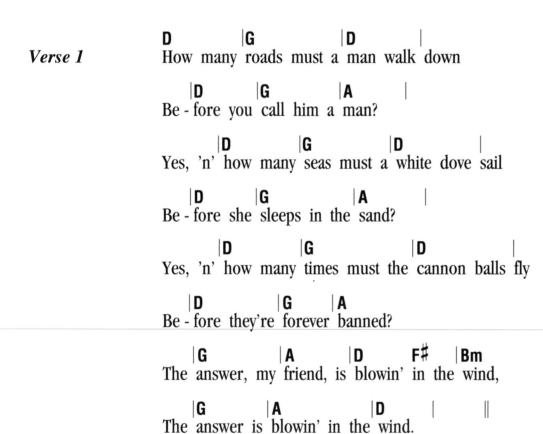

D |**G** |**D** |
How many roads must a man walk down

|**D** |**G** |**A** |
Be - fore you call him a man?

|**D** |**G** |**D** |
Yes, 'n' how many seas must a white dove sail

|**D** |**G** |**A** |
Be - fore she sleeps in the sand?

|**D** |**G** |**D** |
Yes, 'n' how many times must the cannon balls fly

|**D** |**G** |**A**
Be - fore they're forever banned?

|**G** |**A** |**D** |**F♯** |**Bm**
The answer, my friend, is blowin' in the wind,

|**G** |**A** |**D** | ‖
The answer is blowin' in the wind.

Verse 2

D |G |D |
How many times must a man look up

    |D |G |A |
Be - fore he can see the sky?

       |D |G |D |
Yes, 'n' how many ears must one man have

    |D |G |A |
Be - fore he can hear people cry?

      |D |G |D |
Yes, 'n' how many deaths will it take till he knows

    |D |G |A |
That too many people have died?

    |G |A |D   F# |Bm
The answer, my friend, is blowin' in the wind,

   |G |A |D | ‖
The answer is blowin' in the wind.

Verse 3

D |G |D |
How many years can a mountain ex - ist

    |D |G |A |
Be - fore it's washed to the sea?

     |D |G |D |
Yes, 'n' how many years can some people ex - ist

    |D |G |A |
Be - fore they're al - lowed to be free?

     |D |G |D |
Yes, 'n' how many times can a man turn his head,

    |D |G |A |
Pre - tending he just doesn't see?

    |G |A |D   F# |Bm
The answer, my friend, is blowin' in the wind,

   |G |A |D | ‖
The answer is blowin' in the wind.

Catch the Wind

Words and Music by Donovan Leitch

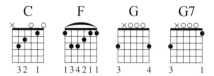

Verse 1

|C | |F |
In the chilly hours and minutes,

|C | |F | |
Of un - certainty, I want to be

C | |F |G |C | |G7 |
In the warm hold of your loving mind.

|C | |F |
To feel you all a - round me,

|C | |F | |
And to take your hand a - long the sand,

C | |F |G |C | |G7 |
Ah, but I may as well try and catch the wind.

Verse 2

```
‖C              |              |F          |
When  sundown      pales  the  sky,

       |C        |        |F            |        |
I  want  to  hide  a - while,  behind  your  smile.

C                |    |F        |G        |C      |      |G7    |
And  everywhere  I'd  look,  your  eyes  I'd  find.

      |C        |              |F          |
For  me  to      love  you  now,

              |C              |F                    |          |
Would  be  the  sweetest  thing,  'twould  make  me  sing,

C          |              |F      |G        |C      |      |G7    |
Ah,  but  I  may  as  well  try  and  catch  the  wind.
```

Verse 3

```
‖C              |              |F          |        |
When  rain  has      hung  the  leaves  with  tears,

C          |      |F        |        |
I  want  you  near  to  kill  my  fears,

C              |              |F      |G        |C      |      |G7    |
To  help  me      to  leave  all  my  blues  be - hind.

      |C        |              |F        |
For  standing      in  your  heart

          |C        |      |F          |        |
Is  where  I  want  to  be,  and  long  to  be,

C          |              |F      |G        |C      |              ‖
Ah,  but  I  may  as  well  try  and  catch  the  wind.
```

The Cruel War Is Raging

American Folksong

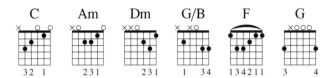

Verse 1

|C |Am |Dm |C   G/B

The cruel war is raging and Johnny has to fight.

|Am |F |G |C   G

I want to be with him from morning till night.

Verse 2

‖C |Am |Dm |C   G/B

I'll go tell your captain, get down upon my knees,

|Am |F |G |C   G

Ten thousand gold guineas I'd give for your release.

Verse 3

‖C |Am |Dm |C   G/B

Ten thousand gold guineas, it grieves my heart so.

|Am |F |G |C   G

Won't you let me go with you? Oh no, my love, no.

Verse 4

‖C |Am |Dm |C   G/B

To - morrow is Sunday and Monday is the day

|Am |F |G |C   G

Your captain calls for you, and you must o - bey.

Verse 5

‖C |Am |Dm |C   G/B

Your captain calls for you, it grieves my heart so.

|Am |F |G |C   G

Won't you let me go with you? Oh no, my love, no.

Verse 6

```
  ||C          |Am        |Dm          |C      G/B
Your waist is too slender, your fingers too small,
    |Am          |F      |G          |C     G
Your cheeks are too rosy to face the cannon - ball.
```

Verse 7

```
  ||C          |Am        |Dm          |C      G/B
Your cheeks are too rosy, it grieves my heart so.
    |Am         |F         |G          |C     G
Won't you let me go with you? Oh no, my love, no.
```

Verse 8

```
  ||C          |Am        |Dm          |C      G/B
Johnny, oh Johnny, I think you are un - kind,
  |Am        |F         |G      |C     G
I love you far better than all other mankind.
```

Verse 9

```
  ||C          |Am        |Dm          |C      G/B
I love you far better than tongue can ex - press.
    |Am         |F         |G          |C     G
Won't you let me go with you? Yes, my love, yes.
```

Verse 10

```
  ||C          |Am        |Dm          |C      G/B
I'll pull back my hair, men's clothes I'll put on,
    |Am         |F         |G          |C     G
I'll pass for your comrade as we march a - long.
```

Verse 11

```
  ||C          |Am        |Dm          |C      G/B
I'll pass for your comrade and none will ever guess.
    |Am         |F         |G          |C       ||
Won't you let me go with you? Yes, my love, yes.
```

Day-O
(The Banana Boat Song)

Words and Music by
Irving Burgie and William Attaway

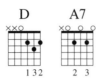

D   A7

Intro

N.C.(D)
Day-o,   day-o.

Daylight come and me wan' go home.

Day, me say day, me say day, me say day, me say day, me say day-o.

Daylight come and me wan' go home.

Verse 1

D
 Work all night on a drink of rum.

D |A7   D
Daylight come and me wan' go home.

D
Stack banana till de morning come.

D |A7   D
Daylight come and me wan' go home.

Verse 2

D |A7
 Come, mister tally man, tally me banana.

D |A7   D
Daylight come and me wan' go home.

D |A7
Come, mister tally man, tally me banana.

D |A7   D
Daylight come and me wan' go home.

Verse 3

‖**D** |　　　　|
Lift six-hand, seven-hand, eight-hand bunch.

D |**A7**　　**D** |
Daylight come and me wan' go home.

D |　　　　|
Six-hand, seven-hand, eight-hand bunch.

D |**A7**　　**D** ‖
Daylight come and me wan' go home.

Chorus

D |　　|
　Day, me say day-o.

D |**A7**　　**D** |
Daylight come and me wan' go home.

D |　　　　|
Day, me say day, me say day, me say…

D |**A7**　　**D**
Daylight come and me wan' go home.

Verse 4

‖**D** |　　　|
A beautiful bunch of ripe banana.

D |**A7**　　**D** |
Daylight come and me wan' go home.

D |　　　|
Hide the deadly black tarantula.

D |**A7**　　**D** ‖
Daylight come and me wan' go home.

Repeat Chorus

Repeat Verse 2

Outro

N.C.(D)|　　|
Day-o,　day-o.

D |**A7**　　**D** |
Daylight come and me wan' go home.

N.C.(D) |　　　　　　　　|　　|
Day,　me say day, me say day, me say day, me say day, me say day-o.

D |**A7**　　**D** ‖
Daylight come and me wan' go home.

Don't Think Twice, It's All Right

Words and Music by Bob Dylan

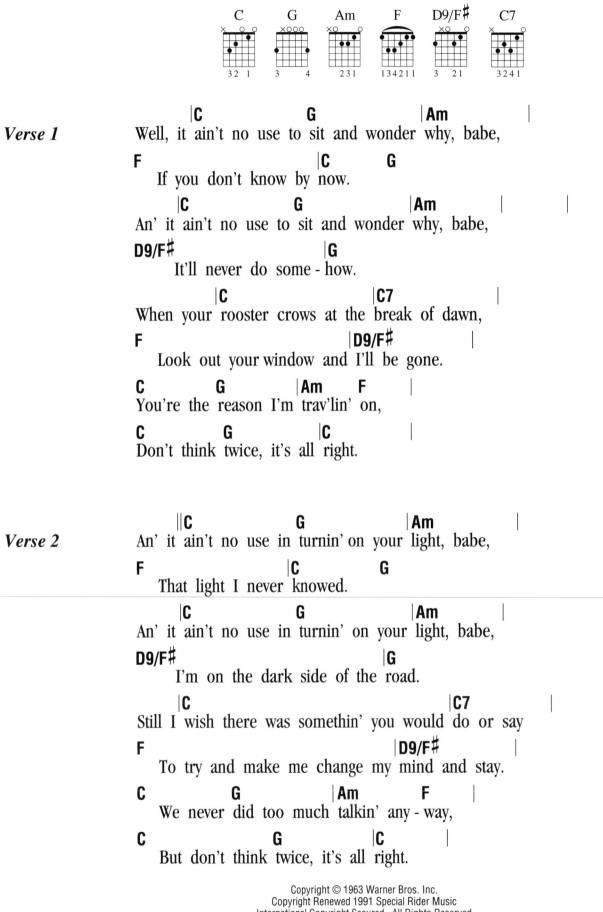

Verse 1

|C   G |Am |
Well, it ain't no use to sit and wonder why, babe,

F |C   G
If you don't know by now.

       |C   G |Am | |
An' it ain't no use to sit and wonder why, babe,

D9/F♯ |G
It'll never do some - how.

         |C |C7 |
When your rooster crows at the break of dawn,

F |D9/F♯ |
Look out your window and I'll be gone.

C   G |Am   F |
You're the reason I'm trav'lin' on,

C   G |C |
Don't think twice, it's all right.

Verse 2

||C   G |Am |
An' it ain't no use in turnin' on your light, babe,

F |C   G
That light I never knowed.

       |C   G |Am |
An' it ain't no use in turnin' on your light, babe,

D9/F♯ |G
I'm on the dark side of the road.

         |C |C7 |
Still I wish there was somethin' you would do or say

F |D9/F♯ |
To try and make me change my mind and stay.

C   G |Am   F |
We never did too much talkin' any - way,

C   G |C |
But don't think twice, it's all right.

STRUM & SING

Verse 3

```
  ||C            G          |Am              |
So it ain't no use in callin' out my name, gal,
 F                          |C       G
   Like you never done be - fore.
     |C            G          |Am            |
An' it ain't no use in callin' out my name, gal,
D9/F#                        |G
    I can't hear you any more.
     |C                       |C7
I'm a - thinkin' and a - wond'rin' walking down the road,
 |F                   |D9/F#
I once loved a woman, a child I'm told.
 |C          G          |Am         F        |
I give her my heart but she wanted my soul,
C            G          |C           |
   But don't think twice, it's all right.
```

Verse 4

```
  ||C   G     |Am
So long,  honey bee,
      |F              |C     G
Where I'm bound, I can't tell.
C      G        |Am          |
Goodbye is too good a word, gal,
D9/F#                    |G          |
   So I'll just say fare - thee - well.
C                |C7
I ain't sayin' you treated me unkind,
  |F                    |D9/F#          |
You could have done better but I don't mind.
C        G        |Am        F        |
   You just kinda wasted my precious time,
C            G          |C          ||
But don't think twice, it's all right.
```

Five Hundred Miles

Words and Music by Hedy West

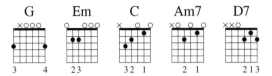

Chorus

|G |Em
If you miss the train I'm on,

|C |Am7
You will know that I am gone.

|D7 | |G
You can hear the whistle blow a hundred miles,

|G |Em
A hundred miles, a hundred miles,

|C |Am7
A hundred miles, a hundred miles,

|D7 | |G |
You can hear the whistle blow a hundred miles.

Verse 1

    ‖**G** |**Em**
Lord, I'm one, Lord, I'm two, Lord,

  |**C** |**Am7**
I'm three, Lord, I'm four, Lord,

  |**D7** | |**G** |
I'm five hundred miles away from home.

    |**G** |**Em**
Away from home, away from home,

    |**C** |**Am7**
Away from home, away from home,

  |**D7** | |**G** |
Lord, I'm five hundred miles away from home.

Verse 2

    ‖**G** |**Em**
Not a shirt on my back,

  |**C** |**Am7**
Not a penny to my name.

    |**D7** | |**G** |
Lord, I can't go back home this - a way.

    |**G** |**Em**
This - a way, this - a way,

    |**C** |**Am7**
This - a way, this - a way,

    |**D7** | |**G** | ‖
Lord, I can't go back home this - a way.

Repeat Chorus

Follow Me

Words and Music by
John Denver

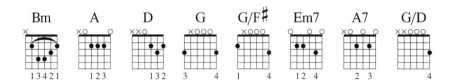

Intro

|**Bm** |**A** |**D**
It's by far the hardest thing I've ever done,

|**G**   **G/F♯** |**Em7** |**A** |**A7**
To be so in love with you and so a-lone.

Chorus

‖**D** |**Em7** |**D** |**G**
Follow me   where I go,   what I do and who I know,

|**D** |**Em7** |**A** |**A7**
Make it part of you to be a part of me.

|**D** |**Em7** |**D** |**G** |
Follow me   up and down,   all the way and all around,

D |**G**   **A7** |**D** |
Take my hand and say you'll follow me.

Verse 1

‖**D** |**A** |**G** |**D**
It's long been on my mind, you know it's been a long, long time,

|**Bm** |**A** |**G** |**A**
I'll try to find the way that I can make you under-stand

|**G** |**D**   **G** |**D**
The way I feel about you and just how much I need you

|**G**   **G/F♯** |**Em7** **G/D** |**G** |**A** |**A7**
To be there where I can talk to you when there's no one else around.

Repeat Chorus

Verse 2

        D   **A**   **G**   **D**

You see, I'd like to share my life with you and show you things I've seen,

Bm   **A**   **G**   **A**

Places that I'm going to, places where I've been

  G   **D**   **G**   **D**

To have you there beside me and never be a-lone

  G   **G/F♯**   **Em7**   **G/D**   **G**   **A**   **A7**

And all the time that you're with me, then we will be at home.

Repeat Chorus

Greenfields

Words and Music by Terry Gilkyson, Richard Dehr and Frank Miller

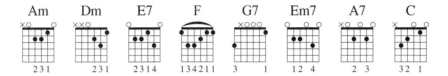

Verse 1

```
Am              Dm        |Am          E7            |
Once there were green fields kissed by the sun.

Am              Dm        |Am          E7          |
Once there were valleys  where  rivers  used  to  run.

F               G7        |Em7              A7        |
Once there was blue sky with white clouds high a - bove.

Dm              G7        |Am        E7          |
Once they were part  of  an  everlasting  love.

Am         Dm        |Am    E7          |Am   Dm  |Am      E7  ||
We  were  the  lovers  who  strolled   through  green  fields.
```

Verse 2

```
Am              Dm        |Am          E7          |
Green  fields  are  gone  now,  parched  by  the  sun,

Am              Dm        |Am          E7           |
Gone  from  the  valleys  where  rivers  used  to  run,

F               G7        |Em7          A7           |
Gone  with  the  cold  wind  that  swept  into  my  heart,

Dm              G7        |Am              E7          |
Gone  with  the  lovers  who  let  their  dreams  de - part.

Am              Dm        |Am   E7
Where  are  the  green  fields  that  we     used  to  roam?
```

Bridge

```
F          G7         |Dm        G7    C       |
I'll never  know what made  you  run a-way.

Dm              G7        |Dm         G7       C      |
How can I keep searching when dark clouds hide the day?

Am                          |F           Dm           |
   I only know there's nothing here for me,

Am            Dm            |            E7
Nothing in this wide world left for me to see.
```

Verse 3

```
   ‖Am        Dm     |Am        E7      |
But I'll keep on waiting 'til you re-turn,

Am          Dm       |Am        E7        |
I'll keep on waiting un-til the day you learn.

F           G7       |Em7          |A7       |
 You can't be happy while your heart's on the roam,

Dm          G7       |Am         E7        |
You can't be happy un-til you bring it home,

Am          Dm            |Am E7       |Am    Dm  |Am        ‖
Home to the green fields and me    once a-gain.
```

Guantanamera

Cuban Folksong

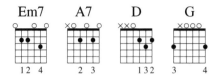

Chorus

|Em7 |A7 |
Guantanamera!   Guajira!

D   **G** |**A7** |
Guantana - mera!

D   **G** |**A7** |
Guantana - me - ra! Guajira!

D   **G** |**A7**
Guantana - me - ra!

Verse 1

‖**G** |**A7**
Yo soy un hombre sincero

|**D**   **G** |**A7**
De donde crece la palma.

|**G** |**A7**
Yo soy un hombre sincero

|**G** |**A7**
De donde crece la palma.

|**D**   **G** |**A7**
Y antes de morirme quie - ro

|**D**   **G** |**A7** ‖
Echar mis versos del al - ma.

Repeat Chorus

Verse 2

        ‖**G** |**A7**
Mi verso es de un verde claro

        |**D**   **G** |**A7**
Y de un car - min encen - dido.

        |**G** |**A7**
Mi verso es de un verde claro

        |**G** |**A7**
Y de un car - min encen - dido.

        |**D**   **G** |**A7**
Mi verso es un cierro heri - do

        |**D**   **G** |**A7** ‖
Que busca en el monte am - pa - ro.

Repeat Chorus

Verse 3

        ‖**G** |**A7**
Con los po - bres de la tierra

        |**D**   **G** |**A7**
Quiero yo mi suerte e - char.

        |**G** |**A7**
Con los po - bres de la tierra

        |**G** |**A7**
Quiero yo mi suerte e - char

        |**D**   **G** |**A7**
El arro - yo de la si - er - ra

        |**D**   **G** |**A7** ‖
Me compla - ce mas que el mar.

Repeat Chorus

House of the Rising Sun

Southern American Folksong

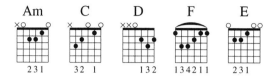

Verse 1

|Am |C |D |F
There is a house in New Orleans

|Am |C |E |
They call the Rising Sun.

|Am |C |D |F
It's been the ruin of many a poor girl,

|Am |E |Am |E
And I, oh Lord, was one.

Verse 2

‖Am |C |D |F
My mother, she is a tailor,

|Am |C |E |
She sells those new blue jeans.

|Am |C |D |F
My sweetheart, he's a drunkard, Lord,

|Am |E |Am |E
Drinks down in New Or - leans.

Verse 3

```
 ‖Am |C       |D       |F
The only thing a drunkard needs

   |Am      |C    |E      |
Is a suitcase and a trunk.

   |Am |C    |D          |F
The only time he's satis - fied

   |Am        |E    |Am    |E  ‖
Is when he's on a drunk.
```

Verse 4

```
 Am          |C    |D          |F
One foot is on the platform,

      |Am       |C    |E    |
And the other one on the train.

   |Am |C     |D       |F
I'm going back to New Or - leans

   |Am        |E     |Am   |E
To wear that ball and chain.
```

Repeat Verse 1

I Can't Help but Wonder (Where I'm Bound)

Words and Music by Tom Paxton

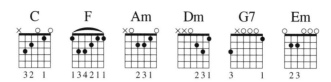

Verse 1

|C |F Am |Dm
It's a long and dusty road, it's a hot and a heavy load,

|G7 | |C
And the folks I meet ain't always kind.

|C
Some are bad and some are good,

|F Am |Dm
Some have done the best they could,

|G7 | |C
Some have tried to ease my troublin' mind.

Chorus

‖Dm |G7
And I can't help but wonder

|C Em |Am
Where I'm bound, where I'm bound.

Dm |G7 |C
Can't help but wonder where I'm bound.

Verse 2

‖C |F Am |Dm
I have wandered through this land just a - doin' the best I can,

|G7 | |C
Tryin' to find what I was meant to do.

|C |F Am |Dm
And the people that I see look as worried as can be

|G7 | |C
And it looks like they are wonderin', too.

Repeat Chorus

Verse 3

‖**C** | |**F** **Am** |**Dm**
Oh, I had a little girl one time, she had lips like sherry wine

|**G7** | |**C** |
And she loved me till my head went plumb in - sane.

|**C** | |**F** **Am** |**Dm**
But I was too blind to see she was driftin' a - way from me

|**G7** | |**C** |
And my good gal went off on the morning train.

Repeat Chorus

Verse 4

‖**C** | |**F** **Am** |**Dm**
And I had a buddy back home but he started out to roam

|**G7** | |**C** |
And I hear he's out by 'Frisco Bay.

|**C** | |**F** **Am** |**Dm**
And some - times when I've had a few, his old voice comes singin' through

|**G7** | |**C** |
And I'm goin' out to see him some old day.

Repeat Chorus

Verse 5

‖**C** | |**F** **Am** |**Dm**
If you see me passing by and you sit and you wonder why,

|**G7** | |**C** |
And you wish that you were a rambler too;

|**C** | |**F** **Am** |**Dm**
Nail your shoes to the kitchen floor, lace 'em up and bar the door,

|**G7** | |**C** | ‖
Thank your stars for the roof that's over you.

I'll Never Find Another You

Words and Music by Tom Springfield

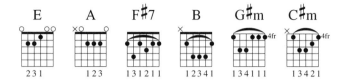

Verse 1

      |E |A
There's a new world somewhere

    |F#7 |B
They call The Promised Land,

     |E |G#m
And I'll be there some day

  |A |B
If you will hold my hand.

   |C#m |A
I still need you there be - side me

  |B   A |G#m
No matter what I do,

A |E   A | B |E   A |E
For I know I'll never find an - other you.

Verse 2

      ‖E |A
There is always someone

  |F#7 |B
For each of us they say,

     |E |G#m
And you'll be my someone

  |A |B
For ever and a day.

   |C#m |A
I could search the whole world over

  |B   A |G#m
Un - til my life is through,

A |E   A | B |E   A |E
But I know I'll never find an - other you.

STRUM & SING

Bridge

     B‖C#m |A
It's a long, long journey,

    |E   B |E
So stay by my side.

     B|C#m |B
When I walk through the storm,

     A |E |B
You'll be my guide.

Verse 3

     ‖E |A
If they gave me a fortune,

   |F#7 |B
My pleasure would be small.

     |E |G#m
I could lose it all to - morrow,

    |A |B
And never mind at all.

    |C#m |A
But if I should lose your love, dear,

  |B   A |G#m
I don't know what I'd do,

A |E   A | B |E A |E   ‖
For I know I'll never find an - other you.

If I Had a Hammer
(The Hammer Song)

Words and Music by Lee Hays and Pete Seeger

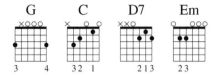

Verse 1

|G |C |G |C
If I had a hammer,   I'd hammer in the morn - ing,

　　　　　|G |C |D7 |
I'd hammer in the evening   all over this land,

　　　　　|G | |Em |
I'd hammer out danger, I'd hammer out a warning,

　　　　　|C   G |C   G |
I'd hammer out love be - tween my brothers and my sisters,

C   G|D7 |G |C |G |
All   over this land.

Verse 2

‖G |C |G |C
If I had a bell,   I'd ring it in the morn - ing,

　　　　　|G |C |D7 |
I'd ring it in the evening   all over this land,

　　　　　|G | |Em |
I'd ring out danger, I'd ring out a warning,

　　　　　|C   G |C   G |
I'd ring out love be - tween my brothers and my sisters,

C   G|D7 |G |C |G |
All   over this land.

Verse 3

‖**G** |**C** |**G** |**C**
If I had a song,   I'd sing it in the morn - ing,

       |**G** |**C** |**D7** |
I'd sing it in the evening all over this land,

    |**G** | |**Em** |
I'd sing out danger, I'd sing out a warning,

    |**C**   **G** |**C**   **G** |
I'd sing out love be - tween my brothers and my sisters,

C **G**|**D7** |**G** |**C** |**G** |
  All   over this land.

Verse 4

‖**G** |**C** |**G** |**C**
Well, I've got a hammer   and I've got a bell,

     |**G** |**C** |**D7** |
And I've got a song to sing all over this land,

      |**G** | |**Em** |
It's the hammer of justice, it's the bell of freedom,

     |**C**   **G** |**C**   **G** |
It's the song about love be - tween my brothers and my sisters,

C **G**|**D7** |**G** |**C** |**G** | ‖
  All   over this land.

Jamaica Farewell

Words and Music by Irving Burgie

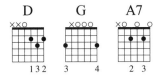

Verse 1

D |G
Down the way where the nights are gay

  |A7 |D |
And the moon shines gaily on the mountaintop,

D |G
I took a trip on a sailing ship,

      |A7 |D
And when I reached Jamaica, I made a stop.

Chorus

  ||D |G |
But I'm sad to say, I'm on my way,

A7 |D
Won't be back for many a day.

  |D |G
My heart is down, my head is turning around.

  |A7 |D |
I had to leave a little crab in Kingston town.

G |A7 |D ||

Verse 2

```
     D                      |G
     Sounds of laughter everywhere,

         |A7               |D              |
     And the dancing fish swaying to and fro.

     D                      |G
     I must declare my heart is there,

             |A7                    |D
     Though I've been from Maine to Mexico.
```

Repeat Chorus

Verse 3

```
     D                      |G                    |
     Under the sea there you can hear Mer folk

     A7                |D              |
     Singing songs that I love so dear.

     D                |G              |A7
     Fish are dancing everywhere and the fun is fine

         |D
     Any time of year.
```

Repeat Chorus

Kisses Sweeter Than Wine

Words by Ronnie Gilbert, Lee Hays, Fred Hellerman and Pete Seeger
Music by Huddie Ledbetter

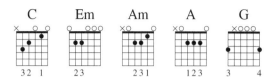

Chorus

C |Em|Am |A | |
Oh,   kisses sweeter than wine,

C |Em|Am |A |
Oh,   kisses sweeter than wine.

Verse 1

‖C   G |Am   Em
When I was a young man and never been kissed,

|G   Em |A
I got to thinkin' over what I had missed.

|C   G |Am   Em |
I got me a girl, kissed her and then,

G   Em |A   ‖
Oh, Lord, I kissed her again.

Repeat Chorus

Verse 2

‖C   G |Am   Em
He asked me to marry and be his sweet wife,

|G   Em |A
And we would be so happy all of our life.

|C   G |Am   Em |
He begged and he pleaded like a natural man and then,

G   Em |A   ‖
Oh Lord, I gave him my hand.

Repeat Chorus

Verse 3
```
      ‖C          G      |Am        Em
I worked mighty hard and so did my wife,

          |G       Em        |A
A - workin' hand in hand to make a good life.

          |C        G      |Am        Em           |
With corn in the fields and wheat in the bins and then,

G    Em           |A                 ‖
Oh Lord, I was the father of twins.
```

Repeat Chorus

Verse 4
```
      ‖C     G      |Am        Em
Our children numbered just about four

          |G      Em         |A
And they all had sweethearts knock on the door.

          |C    G          |Am        Em        |
They all got married and they didn't wait, I was,

G    Em        |A                 ‖
Oh Lord, the grandfather of eight.
```

Repeat Chorus

Verse 5
```
      ‖C     G      |Am     Em
Now we are old and ready to go,

            |G           Em          |A
We get to thinking what happened a long time ago.

          |C       G       |Am       Em       |
We had lots of kids and trouble and pain, but

G    Em        |A              ‖
Oh Lord, we'd do it again.
```

Repeat Chorus

Leaving on a Jet Plane

Words and Music by
John Denver

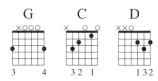

Verse 1

    |G |C
All my bags are packed, I'm ready to go,

    |G |C
I'm standing here out-side your door,

  |G |C |D |
I hate to wake you up to say good-bye.

    |G |C
But the dawn is breakin', it's early morn,

    |G |C
The taxi's waitin', he's blowin' his horn,

 |G |C |D |
Al-ready I'm so lonesome I could die.

Chorus

 ‖G |C |
So kiss me and smile for me,

G |C |
Tell me that you'll wait for me,

G |C |D |
Hold me like you'll never let me go.

    |G |C |G
'Cause I'm leavin' on a jet plane,

       |C |G
Don't know when I'll be back again.

 |C |D | | |
Oh, babe, I hate to go.

Verse 3

‖**D/F#** | |**G** |
It's fare you well,   my own true lover,

|**Em** | |**Am** |
I never ex - pect   to see you a - gain.

|**D/F#** | |**G**
For I'm bound to ride   that northern railroad,

|**Em** | |**Am** |
Perhaps I'll die   upon this train.

Verse 4

‖**D/F#** | |**G** |
You can bury me   in some deep valley,

|**Em** | |**Am** |
For many years   where I may lay,

|**D/F#** | |**G** |
Then you may learn   to love an - other,

|**Em** | |**Am** |
While I am sleep - ing in my grave.

Verse 5

‖**D/F#** | |**G** |
Maybe your friends   think I'm just a stranger,

|**Em** | |**Am** |
My face you nev - er will see no more,

|**D/F#** | |**G** |
But there is one   promise that is given,

|**Em** | |**Am** | ‖
I'll meet you on   God's golden shore.

Michael Row the Boat Ashore

Traditional Folksong

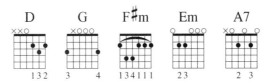

Chorus

|D | |G |D
Michael, row the boat a - shore, Halle - lu - jah!

|F#m |Em |A7 |D
Michael, row the boat a - shore, Halle - lu - jah!

Verse 1

||D | |G |D
Sister, help to trim the sails, Halle - lu - jah!

|F#m |Em |A7 |D
Sister, help to trim the sails, Halle - lu - jah!

Repeat Chorus

Verse 2

||D | |G |D
Jordan River is chilly and cold, Halle - lu - jah!

|F#m |Em |A7 |D
Chills the body but not the soul, Halle - lu - jah!

Repeat Chorus

Verse 3
       ‖D | |G |D

River is deep, and the river is wide, Halle - lu - jah!

       |F♯m |Em |A7 |D

Milk and honey on the other side, Halle - lu - jah!

Repeat Chorus

Verse 4
       ‖D | |G |D

If you get there before I do, Halle - lu - jah!

       |F♯m |Em |A7 |D   ‖

Tell my friends I'm coming too, Halle - lu - jah!

My Ramblin' Boy

Words and Music by Tom Paxton

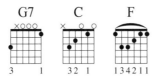

Verse 1

    |**G7** |**C**
He was a man and a friend al - ways,

           |**G7** |**C**
He stuck with me in the hard old days.

      |**C** |
He never cared if I had no dough,

        |**G7** |**C**
We rambled 'round in the rain and snow.

Chorus

      ‖**C**   **F** |**C**
And here's to you my ramblin' boy,

     |**G7** |**C**
May all your ramblin' bring you joy.

     |**C**   **F** |**C**
And here's to you my ramblin' boy,

     |**G7** |**C**
May all your ramblin' bring you joy.

Verse 2
      ‖**G7** |**C**
In Tulsa town we chanced to stray.

          |**G7** |**C**
We thought we'd try to work one day.

        |**C** |
The boss said he had room for one.

        |**G7** |**C**
Says my old pal, "We'd rather bum!"

Repeat Chorus

Verse 3
      ‖**G7** |**C**
Late one night in a jungle camp,

         |**G7** |**C**
The weather it was cold and damp.

       |**C** |
He got the chills and he got 'em bad;

        |**G7** |**C**   ‖
They took the only friend I had.

Repeat Chorus

Verse 4
      ‖**G7** |**C**
He left me there to ramble on,

       |**G7** |**C**
My ramblin' pal is dead and gone.

       |**C** |
If when we die, we go some - where,

       |**G7** |**C**   ‖
I'll bet you a dollar, he's ramblin' there.

Repeat Chorus

Puff the Magic Dragon

Words and Music by
Lenny Lipton and Peter Yarrow

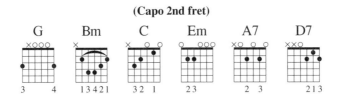

Verse 1

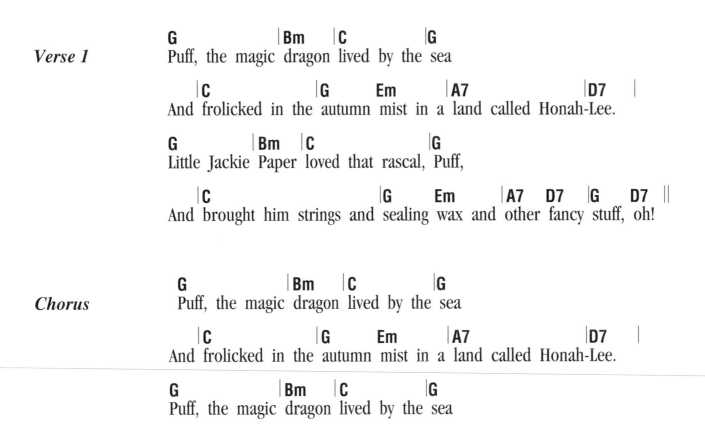

G |Bm |C |G
Puff, the magic dragon lived by the sea

|C |G   Em |A7 |D7 |
And frolicked in the autumn mist in a land called Honah-Lee.

G |Bm |C |G
Little Jackie Paper loved that rascal, Puff,

|C |G   Em |A7   D7 |G   D7 ||
And brought him strings and sealing wax and other fancy stuff, oh!

Chorus

G |Bm |C |G
Puff, the magic dragon lived by the sea

|C |G   Em |A7 |D7 |
And frolicked in the autumn mist in a land called Honah-Lee.

G |Bm |C |G
Puff, the magic dragon lived by the sea

|C |G   Em |A7   D7 |G
And frolicked in the autumn mist in a land called Honah-Lee.

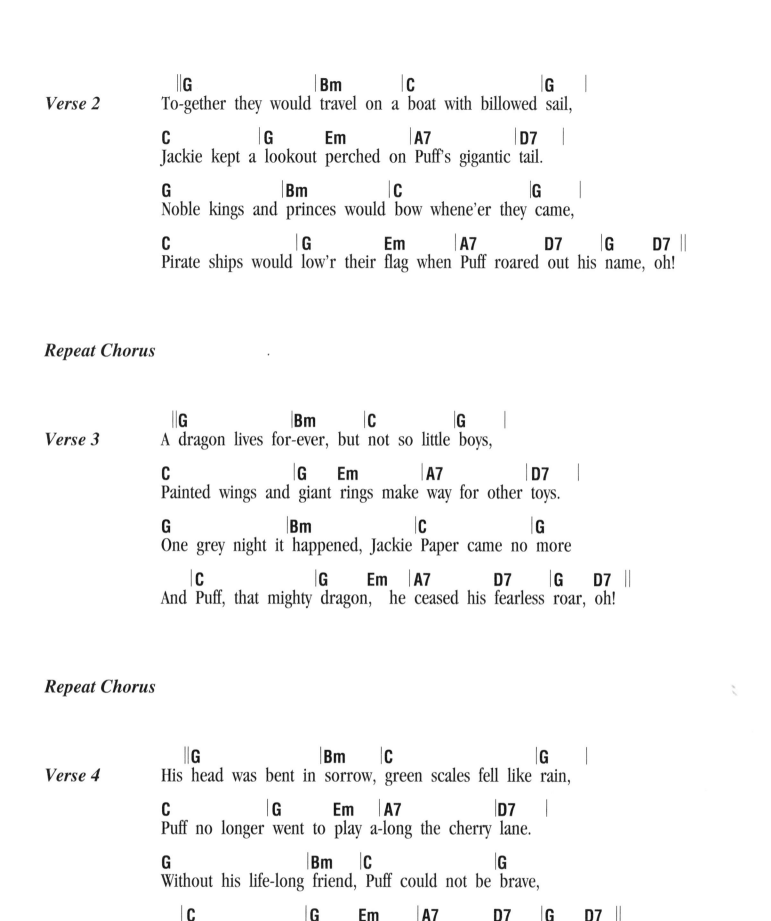

Verse 2

|G |Bm |C |G |
To-gether they would travel on a boat with billowed sail,

C |G   Em |A7 |D7 |
Jackie kept a lookout perched on Puff's gigantic tail.

G |Bm |C |G |
Noble kings and princes would bow whene'er they came,

C |G   Em |A7   D7 |G   D7 ||
Pirate ships would low'r their flag when Puff roared out his name, oh!

Repeat Chorus

Verse 3

|G |Bm |C |G |
A dragon lives for-ever, but not so little boys,

C |G   Em |A7 |D7 |
Painted wings and giant rings make way for other toys.

G |Bm |C |G |
One grey night it happened, Jackie Paper came no more

|C |G   Em |A7   D7 |G   D7 ||
And Puff, that mighty dragon,   he ceased his fearless roar, oh!

Repeat Chorus

Verse 4

|G |Bm |C |G |
His head was bent in sorrow, green scales fell like rain,

C |G   Em |A7 |D7 |
Puff no longer went to play a-long the cherry lane.

G |Bm |C |G |
Without his life-long friend, Puff could not be brave,

|C |G   Em |A7   D7 |G   D7 ||
So Puff, that mighty dragon,   sadly slipped in-to his cave, oh!

Repeat Chorus

Sloop John B.

Traditional

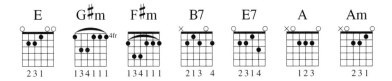

Verse 1

 |**E** |
We come on the sloop John B.,

 |**E** | |
My grandfather and me.

E |**G♯m** |**F♯m** |
'Round Nassau town we did roam.

B7 |**E** |**E7** |**A** |**Am**
   Drinking all night,   we got in a fight,

 |**E** |**B7** |**E** ||
I feel so break up,   I want to go home.

Chorus

 |**E** | |
So hoist up the John B. sails,

E | |
See how the mainsail sets,

E |**G♯m** |**F♯m** |
Call for the captain a - shore, let me go home,

B7 |**E** |**E7** |**A** |**Am**
   Let me go home,   let me go home.

 |**E** |**B7** |**E** ||
I feel so break up,   I want to go home.

Verse 2

```
         |E                        |
         The first mate, oh, he got drunk,

         E                    |        |
         Broke up the people's trunk,

         E              |G♯m             |F♯m   |
         Constable had to come and take him away.

         B7           |E    |E7               |A    |Am
            Sheriff John Stone,    please leave me a - lone,

         |E              |B7             |E      ||
         I feel so break up,    I want to go home.
```

Repeat Chorus

Verse 3

```
         |E                      |    |
         The poor cook, oh, he got fits,

         E          |        |
         Ate up all of the grits,

         E                 |G♯m           |F♯m   |
         Then he took and he ate up all of the corn.

         B7            |E    |E7              |A    |Am
            Sheriff John Stone,    please leave me a - lone,

         |E             |B7            |E      ||
         This is the worst trip    I've ever been on.
```

Sunshine on My Shoulders

Words by John Denver
Music by John Denver, Mike Taylor and Dick Kniss

(Capo 3rd fret)

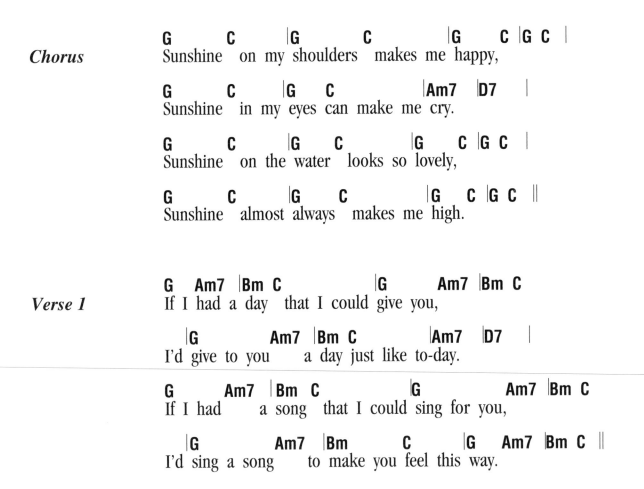

Chorus

G   C |G   C |G   C |G C |
Sunshine   on my shoulders   makes me happy,

G   C |G C |Am7 |D7 |
Sunshine   in my eyes can make me cry.

G   C |G C |G   C |G C |
Sunshine   on the water   looks so lovely,

G   C |G C |G   C |G C ||
Sunshine   almost always   makes me high.

Verse 1

G Am7 |Bm C |G   Am7 |Bm C
If I had a day   that I could give you,

|G   Am7 |Bm C |Am7 |D7 |
I'd give to you   a day just like to-day.

G   Am7 |Bm C |G   Am7 |Bm C
If I had   a song   that I could sing for you,

|G   Am7 |Bm   C |G Am7 |Bm C ||
I'd sing a song   to make you feel this way.

Repeat Chorus

Verse 2

G Am7 |Bm C |G   Am7 |Bm C
If I had a tale that I could tell you,

 |G   Am7|Bm C |Am7 |D7 |
I'd tell a tale   sure to make you smile.

G   Am7 |Bm C |G   Am7 |Bm C
If I had   a wish that I could wish for you,

 |G   Am7 |Bm   C |G   Am7 |Bm C ||
I'd make a wish   for sunshine all the while.

Repeat Chorus

Outro

G   C |G   C |G   Am7 |Bm C |
Sunshine almost all the time makes me high.

G   C |G   C |G Am7 |Bm C G ||
Sunshine almost always…

Suzanne

Words and Music by Leonard Cohen

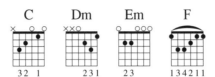

Verse 1

|**C** | |
Su - zanne takes you down to her

C |
Place by the river,

|**Dm** |
You can hear the boats go by.

|**Dm** |
You can spend the night for - ever,

|**C** |
And you know that she's half crazy,

|**C** |
And that's why you want to be there.

|**Em** |
And she feeds you tea and oranges

|**F** |
That came all the way from China.

|**C** |
And just when you want to tell her

|**C** |
That you have no love to give her,

|**Dm** |
She gets you on her wavelength,

|**Dm** |
And lets the river answer

|**C** | | |
That you've always been her lover.

Chorus 1

‖**Em** |
And you want to travel with her,

|**F** |
And you want to travel blind.

|**C** |
And you think you maybe trust her,

|**Dm** | |**C** | | | |
'Cause she's touched your perfect body with her mind.

Verse 2

‖**C** |
And Jesus was a sailor

|**C** |
When he walked upon the water.

|**Dm** |
And he spent a long time watching

|**Dm** |
From a lonely wooden tower.

|**C** |
And when he knew for certain

|**C** |
Only drowning men could see him,

|**Em** |
He said, "All men shall be sailors, then,

|**F** |
Un - til the sea shall free them."

|**C** |
But he himself was broken

|**C** |
Long be - fore the sky would open.

|**Dm** |
For - saken, almost human,

|**Dm** | |**C** | | |
He sank beneath your wisdom like a stone.

Chorus 2

‖**Em**
And you want to travel with him,

|**F**
And you want to travel blind.

|**C** |
And you think maybe you'll trust him,

|**Dm** | |**C** | | |
For he's touched your perfect body with his mind.

Verse 3

‖**C** | |
Su - zanne takes you down to her

C |
Place near the river,

|**Dm** |
You can hear the boats go by.

|**Dm** |
You can spend the night for - ever,

|**C** |
And the sun pours down like honey

|**C** |
On our lady of the harbour.

|**Em** |
And she shows you where to look

|**F** |
Amid the garbage and the flowers.

|**C** |
There are heroes in the seaweed,

|**C** |
There are children in the morning.

|**Dm** |
They are leaning out for love,

|**Dm** |
And they will lean that way for - ever

|**C** | | |
While Suzanne holds her mirror.

Chorus 3

‖**Em** |
And you want to travel with her,

|**F** |
And you want to travel blind.

|**C** |
And you know that you can trust her,

|**Dm** | |**C** | | | ‖
For you've touched her perfect body with your mind.

Teach Your Children

Words and Music by Graham Nash

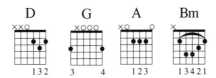

Verse 1

    D |**G**
You who are on the road

         |**D** |**A**
Must have a code that you can live by.

     |**D** |**G**
And so become your - self,

         |**D** |**A** ||
Because the past is just a goodbye.

Chorus 1

    D |**G**
Teach your children well,

         |**D** |**A**
Their father's hell did slowly go by.

     |**D** |**G**
And feed them on your dreams,

           |**D** |**A** |
The one they pick's the one you'll know by.

D |**G**
   Don't you ever ask them why,

                 |**D**
If they told you, you would cry,

            |**Bm** |**G**   **A**
So just look at them and sigh

            |**D** |**G** |**D** |**A**
And know they love you.

Verse 2

      ‖**D** |**G**
And you, of the tender years

               |**D** |**A**
Can't know the fears that your elders grew by.

       |**D** |**G**
And so please help them with your youth,

          |**D** |**A**   ‖
They seek the truth before they can die.

Chorus 2

D |**G**
Teach your parents well,

         |**D** |**A**
Their children's hell did slowly go by.

   |**D** |**G**
And feed them on your dreams,

        |**D** |**A** |
The one they pick's the one you'll know by.

D |**G**
  Don't you ever ask them why,

               |**D**
If they told you, you would cry,

             |**Bm** |**G**   **A**
So just look at them and sigh

         |**D** |**G** |**D** **A** |**D**   ‖
And know they love you.

There but for Fortune

Words and Music by Phil Ochs

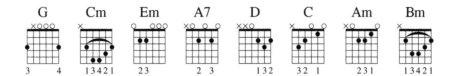

Verse 1

G |Cm |G |Cm |
Show me a prison,   show me a jail,

G |Em |A7 |D
Show me a prisoner whose face has gone pale,

 |G |Em |C |Am
And I'll show you a young man with so many reasons why,

 |Bm |Em |A7 |D ||
And there but for fortune, may go you or I.

Verse 2

G |Cm |G |Cm |
Show me the alley,   show me the train,

G |Em |A7 |D
Show me a hobo who sleeps out in the rain,

 |G |Em |C |Am
And I'll show you a young man with so many reasons why,

Bm |Em |A7 |D ||
There but for fortune, may go you or go I.

Verse 3

```
G            |Cm    |G           |Cm   |
Show me the whiskey stains on the floor,

G            |Em             |A7          |D
Show me the drunken man as he stumbles out the door,

 |G              |Em             |C         |Am
And I'll show you a young man with so many reasons why,

Bm          |Em          |A7       |D      ||
There but for fortune, may go you or go I.
```

Verse 4

```
G            |Cm        |G           |Cm   |
Show me the country where bombs had to fall,

G            |Em     |A7          |D
Show me the ruins of buildings once so tall,

 |G              |Em             |C         |Am
And I'll show you a young land with so many reasons why,

Bm          |Em          |A7       |D       |G      ||
There but for fortune, go you or go I, you and I.
```

This Land Is Your Land

Words and Music by Woody Guthrie

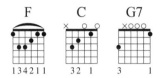

Chorus

       ‖**F** | |**C** |
This land is your land and this land is my land,

  |**G7** | |**C** |
From Cali - fornia to the New York Island,

      |**F** | |**C** | |
From the redwood forest to the Gulf Stream waters,

G7 | |**C** |
This land was made for you and me.

Verse 1

     ‖**F** |**C** |
As I was walking that ribbon of highway,

  |**G7** | |**C** |
I saw a - bove me that endless skyway.

    |**F** | |**C** | |
I saw be - low me that golden valley,

G7 | |**C** |
This land was made for you and me.

Repeat Chorus

Verse 2

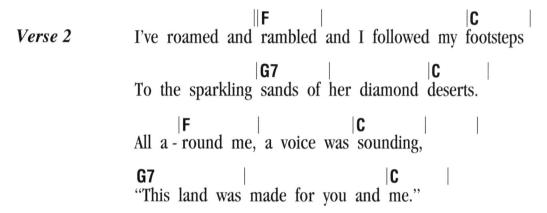

‖ **F** | | **C** |
I've roamed and rambled and I followed my footsteps

|**G7** | |**C** |
To the sparkling sands of her diamond deserts.

|**F** | |**C** | |
All a - round me, a voice was sounding,

G7 | |**C** |
"This land was made for you and me."

Repeat Chorus

Verse 3

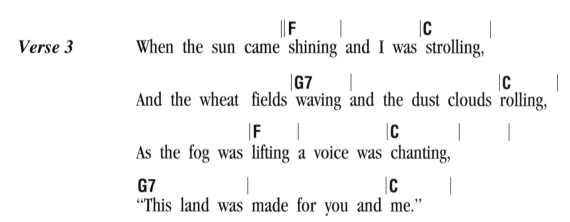

‖ **F** | |**C** |
When the sun came shining and I was strolling,

|**G7** | |**C** |
And the wheat fields waving and the dust clouds rolling,

|**F** | |**C** | |
As the fog was lifting a voice was chanting,

G7 | |**C** |
"This land was made for you and me."

Repeat Chorus

Verse 4

‖**F** | |**C** |
In the shadow of the steeple I saw my people,

|**G7** | |**C** |
By the relief office I seen my people.

|**F** | |**C** | |
As they stood there hungry, I stood there asking,

G7 | |**C** |
"Is this land made for you and me?"

Repeat Chorus

Verse 5

‖**F** | |**C** | |
Nobody living can ever stop me

|**G7** | |**C** |
As I go walking down that freedom highway,

|**F** | |**C** | |
Nobody living can ever make me turn back.

G7 | |**C** | ‖
This land was made for you and me.

The Times They Are a-Changin'

Words and Music by Bob Dylan

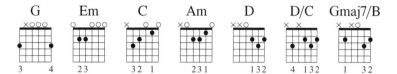

Verse 1

|G |Em |C |G
Come gather 'round people wher - ever you roam

|G |Am |C |D
And ad - mit that the waters a - round you have grown.

|G |Em |C |G |
And ac - cept it that soon you'll be drenched to the bone.

|G |Am |D |
If your time to you is worth savin',

|D |D/C |Gmaj7/B |D
Then you bet - ter start swimmin' or you'll sink like a stone,

|G | |C |D |G |
For the times, they are a - chang - in'.

Verse 2

 ‖G |Em |C |G
Come writers and critics who prophesize with your pen,

 |G |Am |C |D
And keep your eyes wide, the chance won't come again.

 |G |Em |C |G |
And don't speak too soon, for the wheel's still in spin,

 |G |Am |D |
And there's no tellin' who that it's namin'.

 | |D/C |Gmaj7/B |D
For the loser now will be later to win,

 |G | |C |D |G |
For the times, they are a - chang - in'.

 ‖G |Em |C |G
Come senators, congressmen, please heed the call.

Verse 3

 |G |Am |C |D
Don't stand in the doorway, don't block up the hall.

 |G |Em |C |G |
For he that gets hurt will be he who has stalled

 |G |Am |D |
There's a battle out - side and it's ragin'.

 | |D/C |Gmaj7/B |D
It'll soon shake your windows and rattle your walls,

 |G | |C |D |G |
For the times, they are a - chang - in'.

Verse 4

```
  ‖G          |Em    |C              |G
Come mothers and fathers throughout the land

   |G         |Am         |C         |D
And don't criti - cize what you can't under - stand.

    |G              |Em              |C            |G        |
Your sons and your daughters are be - yond your com - mand.

    |G        |Am    |D         |
Your old road is rapidly agin'.

       |              |D/C          |Gmaj7/B      |D
Please get out of the new one if you can't lend your hand,

     |G    |          |C   |D  |G    |
For the times, they are a - chang - in'.
```

Verse 5

```
  ‖G       |Em     |C        |G
The line it is drawn, the curse it is cast.

   |G      |Am    |C     |D
The slow one now will later be fast.

    |G      |Em    |C     |G        |
As the present now will later be past,

   |G       |Am    |D       |
The order is rapidly fadin'.

       |              |D/C       |Gmaj7/B |D
And the first one now will later  be  last,

     |G    |          |C   |D    |G    |      ‖
For the times, they are a - chang - in'.
```

Tom Dooley

Traditional

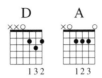

Verse 1

D | |
Hang your head, Tom Dooley,

D |**A** |
Hang your head and cry.

A |
Killed poor Laura Fos - ter.

   |**A** |**D**
You know you bound to die.

Verse 2

   ||**D** |
You took her on the hillside,

  |**D** |**A**
As God Almighty knows.

  |**A** |
You took her on the hillside,

  |**A** |**D**
And there you hid her clothes.

Verse 3

‖**D** |
You took her on the roadside,

|**D** |**A** |
Where you begged to be ex - cused.

|**A** |
You took her by the roadside,

|**A** |**D**
Where there you hid her shoes.

Verse 4

‖**D** |
You took her on the hillside

|**D** |**A** |
To make her be your wife.

|**A** |**A**
You took her on the hillside,

|**A** |**D** ‖
Where there you took her life.

Turn Around

Words and Music by Alan Greene, Malvina Reynolds and Harry Belafonte

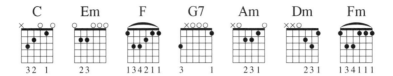

Verse 1

C   **|Em**   **|F**   **|G7** |
Where are you going, my little one, little one?

Am   **|Em**   **|Dm**   **|G7**
Where are you going, my baby, my own?

   |C   **|Em**   **|F**   **|Fm**
Turn a - round and you're two, turn a - round and you're four,

   |C   **|Dm**   **|G7**   **|C**
Turn a - round and you're a young girl going out of the door.

Chorus 1

   ‖C   **|Em**
Turn a - round, turn a - round,

   |F   **|Em**   **|F** **C** **G7** **|C** | ‖
Turn a - round, and you're a young girl going out of the door.

Verse 2

```
        C            |Em       |F         |G7
Where are you going my little one, little one?

        |Am       |Em      |Dm           |G7
Little dirndls and petticoats, where have you gone?

        |C            |Em          |F           |Fm
Turn a - round and you're tiny, turn a - round and you're grown,

        |C            |Dm          |G7          |C
Turn a - round and you're a young wife with babes of your own.
```

Chorus 2

```
        ||C          |Em
Turn a - round, turn a - round,

        |F            |Em          |F    C  G7 |C    ||
Turn a - round, and you're a young wife with babes of your own.
```

Turn! Turn! Turn!
(To Everything There Is a Season)
Words from the Book of Ecclesiastes
Adaptation and Music by Pete Seeger

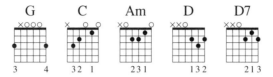

Chorus

|G   C |G Am |
To every - thing, turn, turn, turn,

|G   C |G Am |
There is a season, turn, turn, turn,

|D |D7
And a time to every purpose

|G |
Under heaven.

Verse 1

||D7 |G
A time to be born, a time to die,

|D7 |G
A time to plant, a time to reap,

|D7 |G
A time to kill, a time to heal,

|C |D7 |G |
A time to laugh, a time to weep.

Repeat Chorus

Verse 2

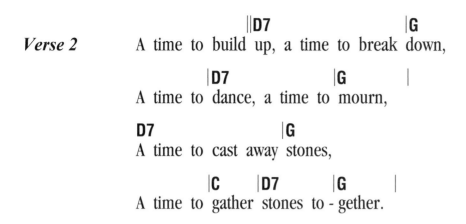

           ‖**D7** |**G**
A time to build up, a time to break down,

     |**D7** |**G** |
A time to dance, a time to mourn,

D7 |**G**
A time to cast away stones,

    |**C** |**D7** |**G** |
A time to gather stones to - gether.

Repeat Chorus

Verse 3

           ‖**D7** |**G**
A time of war, a time of peace,

    |**D7** |**G** |
A time of love, a time of hate,

D7 |**G**
A time you may em - brace,

 |**C** |**D7** |**G** |
A time to re - frain from em - bracing.

Repeat Chorus

Verse 4

           ‖**D7** |**G**
A time to gain, a time to lose,

     |**D7** |**G**
A time to rend, a time to sew,

     |**D7** |**G**
A time of love, a time of hate,

    |**C** |**D7** |**G** | ‖
A time for peace, I swear it's not too late.

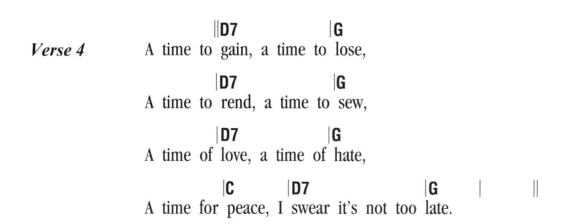

Walk Right In

Words and Music by Gus Cannon and H. Woods

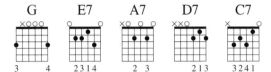

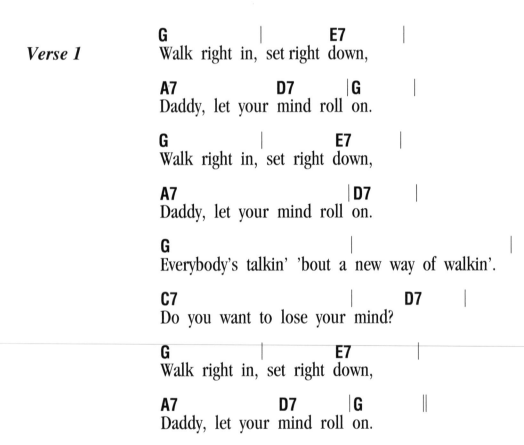

Verse 1

G | **E7** |
Walk right in, set right down,

A7 **D7** |**G** |
Daddy, let your mind roll on.

G | **E7** |
Walk right in, set right down,

A7 |**D7** |
Daddy, let your mind roll on.

G | |
Everybody's talkin' 'bout a new way of walkin'.

C7 | **D7** |
Do you want to lose your mind?

G | **E7** |
Walk right in, set right down,

A7 **D7** |**G** ||
Daddy, let your mind roll on.

Verse 2

```
G                    |        E7         |
Walk right in, set right down,

A7          D7       |G          |
Baby, let your hair hang down.

G                    |        E7         |
Walk right in, set right down,

A7                   |D7         |
Baby, let your hair hang down.

G                                |                          |
Everybody's talkin' 'bout a new way of walkin'.

C7                          |        D7   |
Do you want to lose your mind?

G                    |        E7         |
Walk right in, set right down,

A7          D7       |G     E7      |
Baby, let your hair hang down.

A7          D7       |G          ||
Baby, let your hair hang down.
```

We Shall Overcome

Words based on 1901 hymn by C. Albert Findley entitled "I'll Overcome Some Day"
Music based on 1794 hymn entitled "O Sanctissima"

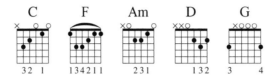

Verse 1

```
     C       F    |C   |          F    |C      |
We shall over - come, we shall over - come,

     C       F    |Am  D  |G      D  |G
We shall over - come some day,

        |C   F  |C   |F G  |Am      |
Oh, deep  in my heart, I do be - lieve,

     C       F    |C   G  |C   F  |C      ||
We shall over - come some day.
```

Verse 2

```
     C        F     |C   |          F     |C      |
We'll walk hand in hand, we'll walk hand in hand,

     C        F     |Am  D  |G     D  |G
We'll walk hand in hand some day,

        |C   F  |C   |F G  |Am      |
Oh, deep  in my heart, I do be - lieve,

     C       F    |C   G  |C   F  |C      ||
We shall over - come some day.
```

Verse 3

```
C       F    |C   |      F    |C       |
We  are  not  a - fraid,  we  are  not  a - fraid,

C       F    |Am  D |G    D    |G
We  are  not  a - fraid  to - day,

   |C   F    |C   |F G      |Am      |
Oh,  deep  in  my  heart,  I  do  be - lieve,

C       F    |C   G  |C   F  |C       ||
We  shall  over - come  some  day.
```

Verse 4

```
C       F    |C      |      F    |C       |
We  shall  stand  to - gether,  we  shall  stand  to - gether,

C       F    |Am  D |G    D    |G
We  shall  stand  to - geth - er  now,

   |C   F    |C   |F G      |Am      |
Oh,  deep  in  my  heart,  I  do  be - lieve,

C       F    |C   G  |C   F  |C       ||
We  shall  over - come  some  day.
```

Will the Circle Be Unbroken

Words by Ada R. Habershon
Music by Charles H. Gabriel

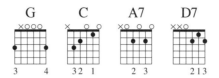

Verse 1

|G |
I was standing by my window

|C |G
On one cold and cloudy day,

|G |
When I saw the hearse come rollin'

|A7 |D7
For to take my mother a - way.

Chorus

‖G |
Will the circle be un - broken

|C |G
By and by Lord, by and by?

|C |G
There's a better home a - waiting

|D7 |G |
In the sky, in the sky.

Verse 2

    ‖**G** |
Oh, I told the under - taker,

      |**C** |**G**
"Under - taker, please drive slow,

      |**G** |
For this body you are hauling,

     |**A7** |**D7**
Lord, I hate to see her go."

Repeat Chorus

Verse 3

    ‖**G** |
I will follow close be - hind her,

     |**C** |**G**
Try to hold up and be brave,

     |**G** |
But I could not hide my sorrow

      |**A7** |**D7**   ‖
When they laid her in the grave.

Repeat Chorus

American Pie

Words and Music by Don McLean

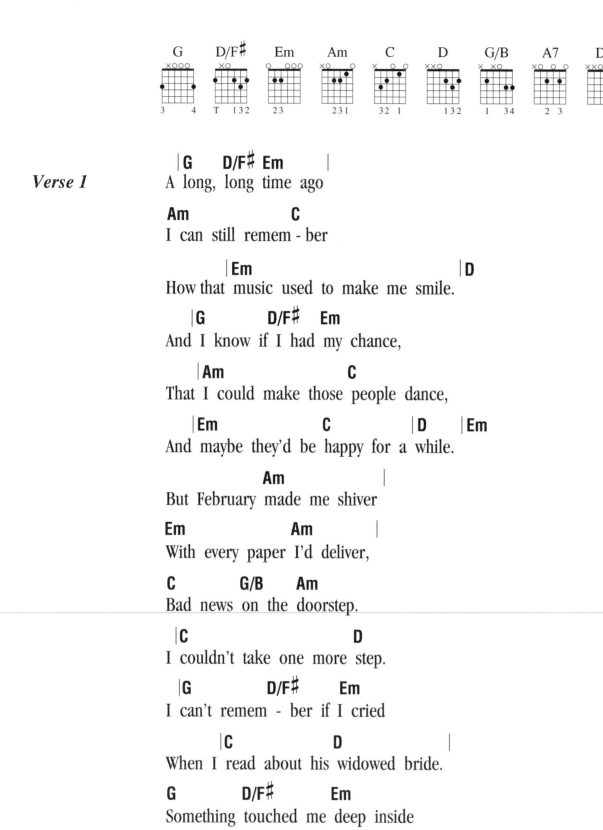

| G | D/F# | Em | Am | C | D | G/B | A7 | D7 |

Verse 1

|G   D/F# Em |
A long, long time ago

Am   C
I can still remem - ber

      |**Em** |**D**
How that music used to make me smile.

   |**G**   **D/F#**   **Em**
And I know if I had my chance,

    |**Am**   **C**
That I could make those people dance,

   |**Em**   **C** |**D** |**Em**
And maybe they'd be happy for a while.

       Am |
But February made me shiver

Em   **Am** |
With every paper I'd deliver,

C   **G/B**   **Am**
Bad news on the doorstep.

 |**C**   **D**
I couldn't take one more step.

 |**G**   **D/F#**   **Em**
I can't remem - ber if I cried

   |**C**   **D** |
When I read about his widowed bride.

G   **D/F#**   **Em**
Something touched me deep inside

 |**C** **D** |**G** | ||
The day the music died. So…

Chorus

```
    G   C           |G          D
Bye, bye, Miss A - merican Pie.
        |G          C           |G          D
Drove my Chevy to the levee, but the levee was dry.
        |G          C           |G              D
And them good ol' boys were drinking whiskey and rye,
        |Em                    |A7      |
Singing, "This'll be the day that I die,
Em                         |D    |        ||
This'll be the day that I die."
```

Verse 2

```
    G               |Am
Did you write the book of love,
        |C          |Am         |Em
And do you have faith in God above
                |D7         |
If the Bible tells you so?
        |G      D/F♯ |Em
Now, do you believe  in  rock 'n' roll?
    |Am             |C
Can music save your mortal soul?
    |Em                |A7                 |D7      |
And can you teach me how to dance real slow?
        |Em                |D
Well, I know that you're in love with him
        |Em               |D7
'Cause I saw you dancing in the gym.
    |C          G           |Am
You both kicked off your shoes.
```

```
                  |C                                  |D7
     Man,  I  dig  those  rhythmic  blues.
                  |G          D/F♯    |Em
     I  was  a  lonely  teen - age  broncin'  buck
               |Am                          |C
     With  a  pink  carnation  and  a  pickup  truck.
            |G          D/F♯      |Em
     But  I  knew  I  was  out  of  luck
                  |C            |D7      |G    C    |
     The  day  the  mu - sic  died.
     G          D                   ‖
     I  started  singing…
```

Repeat Chorus

Verse 3
```
                     |G                          |Am
     Now,  for  ten  years  we've  been  on  our  own,
            |C                          |Am            |Em
     And  moss  grows  fat  on  a  rolling  stone.
                          |D7                  |
     But  that's  not  how  it  used  to  be
                  |G      D/F♯        |Em
     When  the  jester  sang  for  the  king  and  queen
            |Am                  |C
     In  a  coat  he  borrowed  from  James  Dean,
            |Em                      |A7            |D7        |
     And  a  voice  that  came  from  you  and  me.
               |Em                      |D
     Oh,  and  while  the  king  was  looking  down,
            |Em                  |D7
     The  jester  stole  his  thorny  crown.
            |C                          G        |Am
     The  courtroom  was  ad - journed,
```

```
|C                        |D7
No verdict was returned.

       |G      D/F♯  |Em
And while Lenin read a book on Marx,

  |Am               |C
A quartet practiced in the park,

     |G         D/F♯ |Em
And we sang dirges in the dark

        |C          |D7        |G    C|
The day the mu - sic died.

G         D              ‖
We were singin'…
```

Repeat Chorus

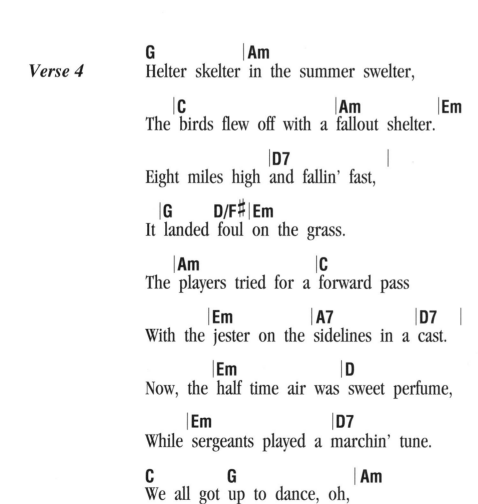

```
           G          |Am
Verse 4    Helter skelter in the summer swelter,

            |C                    |Am          |Em
           The birds flew off with a fallout shelter.

                        |D7                 |
           Eight miles high and fallin' fast,

            |G      D/F♯|Em
           It landed foul on the grass.

             |Am                |C
           The players tried for a forward pass

               |Em          |A7          |D7    |
           With the jester on the sidelines in a cast.

               |Em                 |D
           Now, the half time air was sweet perfume,

               |Em                |D7
           While sergeants played a marchin' tune.

           C          G              |Am
           We all got up to dance, oh,
```

```
        |C                      |D7
But  we  never  got  the  chance.

            |G      D/F♯  |Em
'Cause  the  players  tried  to  take  the  field,

      |Am              |C
The  marching  band  re - fused  to  yield.

        |G        D/F♯  |Em
Do  you  re - call  what  was  revealed

          |C      |D7          |G    C|
The  day  the  music  died?

G            D            ‖
We  started  singin'…
```

Repeat Chorus

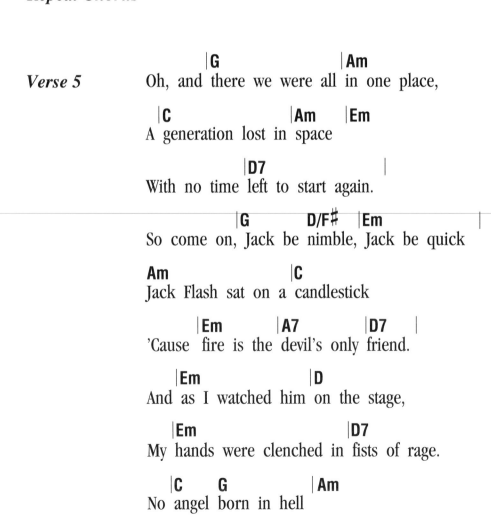

```
                |G                |Am
Oh,  and  there  we  were  all  in  one  place,

      |C              |Am    |Em
A  generation  lost  in  space

            |D7                    |
With  no  time  left  to  start  again.

                |G        D/F♯  |Em              |
So  come  on,  Jack  be  nimble,  Jack  be  quick

Am              |C
Jack  Flash  sat  on  a  candlestick

      |Em        |A7          |D7      |
'Cause  fire  is  the  devil's  only  friend.

      |Em              |D
And  as  I  watched  him  on  the  stage,

      |Em              |D7
My  hands  were  clenched  in  fists  of  rage.

      |C    G          |Am
No  angel  born  in  hell
```

Verse 5

```
           |C                          |D7
Could break that Satan's spell.

               |G            D/F♯    |Em
And as the flames climbed high in-to the night,

       |Am                  |C
To light the sacrificial rite,

    |G          D/F♯     |Em
I saw Satan  laughing with delight

            |C           |D7    |G     C|
The day the mu-sic died

G          D                |‖
He was singing…
```

Repeat Chorus

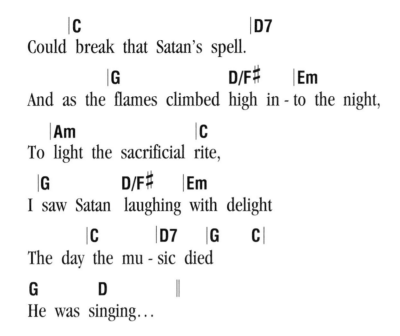

```
                G         D/F♯     Em
Verse 6         I met a girl who sang the blues,

                   |Am                  C
                And I asked her for some happy news

                   |Em                      |D       |
                But she just smiled and turned away.

                G         D/F♯        Em
                I went  down to the sacred store

                G/B       |Am            G/B C
                Where I'd heard the music   years before.

                    |Em              C           |D
                But the man there said the music wouldn't play.

                   |Em              Am
                And in the streets, the children screamed,

                   |Em                    Am
                The lovers cried, and the poets dreamed.

                   |C          G/B  Am     G/B
                But not a word  was spoken,
```

```
 |C                      D
The church bells all were broken,

       |G/B       D/F#    Em      G/B
And the three men I admire most,

     |C                      D
The Father, Son, and the Holy Ghost,

     |G          D/F#     Em
They caught the last train for the coast

     |C       D     |G       |
The day the music died.

G                 D              ||
And they were singing…
```

Repeat Chorus

Kumbayah

Congo Folksong

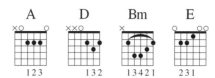

Verse 1

‖ **A** | **D** | **A** |
Kumba - yah, my Lord,   Kumba - yah.

| **A** | **Bm** | **E** |
Kumba - yah, my Lord,   Kumba - yah.

| **A** | **D** | **A** |
Kumba - yah, my Lord,   Kumba - yah.

Bm | **A**   **E** | **A** |
Oh   Lord, Kumba - yah.

Verse 2

‖ **A** | **D** | **A** |
Someone's crying, Lord,   Kumba - yah.

| **A** | **Bm** | **E** |
Someone's crying, Lord,   Kumba - yah.

| **A** | **D** | **A** |
Someone's crying, Lord,   Kumba - yah.

Bm | **A**   **E** | **A** |
Oh   Lord, Kumba - yah.

Verse 3

‖ **A** | **D** | **A** |
Someone's singing, Lord,   Kumba - yah.

| **A** | **Bm** | **E** |
Someone's singing, Lord,   Kumba - yah.

| **A** | **D** | **A** |
Someone's singing, Lord,   Kumba - yah.

Bm | **A**   **E** | **A** | ‖
Oh   Lord, Kumba - yah.

The Marvelous Toy

Words and Music by Tom Paxton

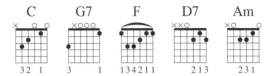

Verse 1

      |C |G7 |C |G7
When I was just a wee little lad full of health and joy,

      |F |C |D7 |G7
My father homeward came one night and gave to me a toy.

     |C |G7 |C |F
A wonder to be - hold, it was, with many colors bright,

       |F |C   Am |D7 |G7
And the moment I laid eyes on it, it be - came my heart's de - light.

Chorus 1

      ‖C |G7
It went "zip" when it moved and "bop" when it stopped,

     |C |F
And "whirr" when it stood still.

   |F |C |G7 |C G7
I never knew just what it was and I guess I never will.

Verse 2

```
  ‖C              |G7              |C              |G7
The first time that I picked it up, I had a big sur - prise,

   |F                        |C                           |
For  right on its bottom were two big buttons that

D7                    |G7
Looked like big green eyes.

   |C                       |G7                    |C              |F
I first pushed one and then the other, and then I twisted its lid,

   |F              |C    Am  |D7              |G7
And when I set it down a - gain, this is what it did:
```

Repeat Chorus 1

Verse 3

```
   ‖C                      |G7
It first marched left and then marched right,

   |C                      |G7
And then marched under a chair.

   |F                      |C              |D7          |G7
And when I looked where it had gone, it wasn't even there.

   |C                      |G7                    |C              |F
I started to sob and my daddy laughed, for he knew that I would find,

   |F                      |C    Am  |D7              |G7
When I turned around, my marvelous toy, chugging from be - hind.
```

Repeat Chorus 1

Verse 4

|| C | G7

Well, the years have gone by too quickly, it seems,

| C | G7

I have my own little boy.

| F | C | D7 | G7

And yesterday I gave to him my marvelous little toy.

| C | G7

His eyes nearly popped right out of his head,

| C | F

And he gave a squeal of glee.

| F | C   Am

Neither one of us knows just what it is,

| D7 | G7

But he loves it, just like me.

Chorus 2

|| C | G7

It still goes "zip" when it moves, and "bop" when it stops,

| C | F

And "whirr" when it stands still.

| F | C

I never knew just what it was,

| G7 | C ||

And I guess I never will.

Scarborough Fair

Traditional English

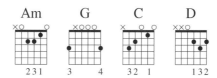

Verse 1

|**Am** | | |**G** |**Am** | | |
Are you going to Scarborough Fair?

C |**Am** |**D** |**Am** |
Parsley, sage, rose - mary, and thyme.

|**Am** |**C** | |**G** |
Re - member me to one who lives there,

|**Am** |**D** |**G** |**Am** | ‖
For she was once a true love of mine.

Verse 2

|**Am** | |**G** |**Am** | |
Tell her to make me a cambric shirt,

C |**Am** |**D** |**Am** |
Parsley, sage, rose - mary, and thyme,

|**Am** |**C** | |**G** |
With - out any seam or fine needle - work,

|**Am** |**D** |**G** |**Am** | ‖
For she was once a true love of mine.

Verse 3

```
Am          |          |G      |Am  |      |
Tell her to wash it in yonder dry well,

C      |Am      |D      |Am      |
 Parsley, sage, rose - mary, and thyme,

   |Am        |C        |          |G      |
Where water ne'er sprung, nor drop of rain fell,

   |Am    |D    |G        |Am  |      ||
For she was once a true love of mine.
```

Verse 4

```
Am          |          |G      |Am  |      |
Tell her to dry it on yonder thorn,

C      |Am      |D      |Am      |
 Parsley, sage, rose - mary, and thyme,

   |Am        |C        |          |G      |
Which never bore blossom since Adam was born,

   |Am    |D    |G        |Am  |      ||
For she was once a true love of mine.
```

Verse 5

```
Am          |          |G      |Am  |      |
Will you find me an acre of land,

C      |Am      |D      |Am      |
 Parsley, sage, rose - mary, and thyme,

   |Am        |C    |          |G      |
Be - tween the sea foam and the sea sand,

   |Am    |D    |G        |Am  |      ||
For she was once a true love of mine.
```

Verse 6

```
Am          |            |G    |Am    |        |
Will you plow it with a lamb's horn,

C      |Am       |D        |Am     |
  Parsley, sage, rose - mary, and thyme,

  |Am      |C        |              |G      |
And sow it all over with one pepper - corn,

  |Am      |D    |G        |Am     |      ||
For she was once a true love of mine.
```

Verse 7

```
Am          |            |G    |Am    |        |
Will you reap it with sickle of leather,

C      |Am       |D        |Am     |
  Parsley, sage, rose - mary, and thyme,

  |Am      |C        |              |G      |
And tie it all up with a peacock's feather,

  |Am      |D    |G        |Am     |      ||
For she was once a true love of mine.
```

Verse 8

```
Am            |          |G        |Am    |        |
When you've done and finished your work,

C      |Am       |D        |Am     |
  Parsley, sage, rose - mary, and thyme,

  |Am      |C        |              |G      |
Then come to me for your cambric shirt,

  |Am      |D    |G        |Am     |      ||
And you shall be a true love of mine.
```

The Unicorn

Words and Music by Shel Silverstein

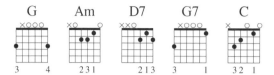

Verse 1

|G |Am
A long time ago, when the earth was green,

           |D7 |G
There was more kinds of animals than you've ever seen,

         |G   G7 |C
And they'd run around free while the earth was being born,

         |G |D7 G |
And the loveliest of all was the uni - corn.

Chorus 1

         ‖G |Am |
There was green alligators and long - necked geese,

D7 |G |
Hump - back camels and chimpanzees,

G   G7 |C
Cats and rats and elephants, but sure as you're born,

      |G |D7 G |
The loveliest of all was the uni - corn.

Verse 2

```
       ‖G                         |Am
Lord seen some sinnin' and it caused him pain.

    |D7                      |G
He says, "Stand back, I'm gonna make it rain.

    |G          G7      |C
So hey, Brother Noah, I'll tell you what to do,

       |G           D7    |G
Go and build me a floating zoo."
```

Chorus 2

```
                ‖G                      |Am
"And you take two alligators and a couple of geese,

    |D7                           |G
Two hump - back camels and two chimpanzees,

    |G                G7           |C
Two cats, two rats, two elephants, but sure as you're born,

    |G                   |D7  G      |
Noah, don't you forget my uni - corns."
```

Verse 3

```
       ‖G                      |Am
Now, Noah was there and he answered the callin'

    |D7                           |G
And he finished up the ark as the rain started fallin',

    |G                G7      |C
Then he marched in the animals two by two,

    |G        D7         |G
And he sung as they went  through:
```

Chorus 3

```
                  ‖G                         |Am
"Hey, Lord, I've got you two alligators and a couple of geese,

    |D7                           |G
Two hump - back camels and two chimpanzees,

    |G                G7            |C
Two cats, two rats, two elephants, but sure as you're born,

    |G                   |D7  G      |
Lord, I just don't see your uni - corns."
```

Verse 4

```
       ‖G                              |Am
Well, Noah looked out through the drivin' rain,

      |D7              |G
But the unicorns was hidin', playin' silly games,

       |G           G7              |C            |
They were kickin' and a-splashin' while the rain was pourin',

G                 |D7  G       |
Oh, them foolish uni - corns.
```

Chorus 4

```
       ‖G                        |Am
I mean the two alligators and a couple of geese,

    |D7                      |G            |
The hump - back camels and the chimpanzees,

       |G        G7           |C
Noah cried, "Close the door 'cause the rain is pourin',

       |G                     |D7  G       |
And we just can't wait for them uni - corns."
```

Verse 5

```
      ‖G                            |Am
And then the ark started movin' and it drifted with the tide,

    |D7                      |G
And the unicorns looked up from the rock and cried,

     |G        G7           |C
And the water came up and sort of floated them away,

     |G                      |D7        G        |
That's why you've never seen a uni - corn to this day.
```

Chorus 5

```
      ‖G                        |Am
You'll see a lot of alligators and a whole mess of geese,

      |D7                  |G
You'll see hump - back camels and chimpanzees,

      |G           G7          |C
You'll see cats and rats and elephants, but sure as you're born,

    |G             |D7  G     |          ‖
You're never gonna see no uni - corn.
```

Where Have All the Flowers Gone?

Words and Music by Pete Seeger

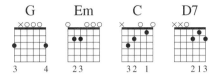

Verse 1

G   **|Em**   **|**
Where have all the flowers gone?

C   **|D7**   **|**
Long time passing.

G   **|Em**   **|**
Where have all the flowers gone?

C   **|D7**   **|**
Long time a - go

G   **|Em**   **|**
Where have all the flowers gone?

C   **|D7**   **|**
Young girls picked them every one.

C   **|G**   **|**
When will they ever learn?

C   **|D7 |G**   **|**   **||**
When will they ever learn?

Verse 2

G |Em |
Where have all the young girls gone?

C |D7 |
Long time passing.

G |Em |
Where have all the young girls gone?

C |D7 |
Long time a - go.

G |Em |
Where have all the young girls gone?

C |D7 |
Taken husbands every one.

C |G |
When will they ever learn?

C |D7 |G | ‖
When will they ever learn?

Verse 3

G |Em |
Where have all the young men gone?

C |D7 |
Long time passing.

G |Em |
Where have all the young men gone?

C |D7 |
Long time a - go.

G |Em |
Where have all the young men gone?

C |D7 |
Gone for soldiers every one.

C |G |
When will they ever learn?

C |D7 |G | ‖
When will they ever learn?

Verse 4

```
G                    |Em              |
Where have all the soldiers gone?

C           |D7          |
Long  time  passing.

G                    |Em              |
Where have all the soldiers gone?

C               |D7        |
Long  time  a - go.

G                    |Em              |
Where have all the soldiers gone?

C                    |D7          |
Gone  to  graveyards  every  one.

C             |G            |
When  will  they  ever  learn?

C              |D7  |G      |      ||
When  will  they  ever  learn?
```

Verse 5

```
G                    |Em              |
Where have all the graveyards gone?

C           |D7          |
Long  time  passing.

G                    |Em              |
Where have all the graveyards gone?

C           |D7        |
Long  time  a - go.

G                    |Em              |
Where have all the graveyards gone?

C                    |D7          |
Covered  with  flowers  every  one.

C             |G            |
When  will  we  ever  learn?

C              |D7  |G      |      ||
When  will  we  ever  learn?
```

Repeat Verse 1

More Great Piano/Vocal Books

FROM CHERRY LANE

For a complete listing of Cherry Lane titles available,
including contents listings, please visit our web site at

www.cherrylane.com

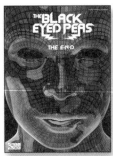

See your local music dealer or contact:

cherry lane
music company

EXCLUSIVELY DISTRIBUTED BY
HAL•LEONARD® CORPORATION

7777 W. BLUEMOUND RD. P.O. BOX 13819 MILWAUKEE, WI 53213

Prices, contents and availability subject to change without notice.

1112